HACK YOUR MIND

How to Harness Your Inner Emotional Resilience for a Positive Life

MANNING L. CROMER

HACK YOUR MIND

Table of Content

About the Book

We humans can be quite indecisive and unstable when our emotions are involved. The human mind is continually racing and ravaged with different thoughts, and these can leave one confused on how to act, when to act, and how to make decisions. Hence, the importance of understanding how our emotions work, where they come from, and how to express them.

Emotions are physiological states that involve three phases. These phases premeditate our psychological environment that tells how we interact with our environment. Life can get pretty crazy at times, leaving us engulfed in a tornado of many challenging events.

The events we let demoralize us and how we handle them is dependent on our emotional resilience. To put it plainly, our emotional resilience is what stands in the gap and keeps us from losing it, especially when it seems like everything is falling apart.

Most times, it's not what life throws at us that gets us irritated or lets us spin out of control; in most cases, it's the way we handle these situations or curveballs is that decides how we react to them. Emotional resilience is the mental build-up that enables us with the strength to withstand whatever life throws at us and how we respond to it. It's our medium of solace in this world filled with turmoil, more or less like our shield against life's missiles, our emotional resilience is.

But, how do we get to the state of emotional resilience? How do you gain control?

Manning Cromer repeatedly thought of these questions and came up with a simple guide to achieving emotional resilience. This book will bring you more understanding on how to cope resiliently no matter what life throws at you, no matter the turmoil you're in. This book is fully detailed to help you understand your emotions, how to help you channel them and how you can be better off by being emotionally resilient.

We will first establish our understanding of emotions. How we interpret them is vital to building our emotional stability. Then we look at how we can develop and increase our resilience capacity using tools or skills that are important to our journey in attaining emotional strength to help us cope with catastrophes as they come.

Introduction

Have you ever been in a situation when it seems as though the world is against you? When it's almost like you cannot get anything right?

You're not alone.

At some point in our lives, we've come across some of life's hiccups - like accidentally spilling hot coffee on your favorite shirt on your way to an interview, forgetting your bank login id when you are in desperate need of cash, rushing out of your home with the wrong briefcase in a rush to meet up with your already late schedule, continually getting into relationships that do not work out, and many others.

These hiccups can cause a cascade of events in our nervous system and send a stream of impulses to our body, urging us to respond in a manner deemed fit by our body's stimuli response. These events test our coping ability daily, and how we respond determines whether we grow as individuals.

When events like this come our way, in most cases by default, we are pushed to say things like "you clumsy klutz," or" I just knew it, it was too good to be true," or we question our sense of judgment. What makes us better is how to suck it up, pick ourselves up, and face whatever we have to face.

Yes, I know it can be challenging. But do you know who can be tougher?

You. Yes, you!

It is said that "when life gives you lemons, you make lemonade." Hiccups don't just come our way for no reason; there is always a price for every win. The more we grow, we don't experience just hiccups.

Life tends to throw adversities and troubles our way. These can be significant events that could shake our compartment and togetherness and desolate our emotional stability - events like losing a loved one, getting fired from a job, being cheated on by a spouse, getting a late mortgage notice, or even losing a house.

When faced with events like this, we survive by digging deep into our sense of balance, our inner reservoir of self-preservation, tapping into memories of times when we coped while also tapping energy off close friends or loved ones.

But digging deep into our reservoir of emotional balance, trying to secure our center and maintain sanity, especially in a situation where all these events are sporadically happening at the same time, we begin to perceive that we are less capable, less skilled, we aren't good enough, or we are not worthy of being helped.

How in the world do you dig deep into a reservoir that is so depleted? How do you find a center that you can barely feel? How in the world would you handle such traumas when you can barely stay afloat?

By strengthening your Resilience.

We overcome life hiccups and spiral disasters by strengthening our emotional resilience.

This book will shed light on how to cope resiliently no matter what life may throw at us, regardless of the level of turmoil to our resilience we're facing.

We will first establish our understanding of emotions. How we interpret them is vital to building our emotional stability. Then we look at how we can develop and increase our resilience capacity using tools or skills that are important to our journey on attaining emotional strength to help us cope with catastrophes as they come.

Part I

Understanding Emotions

CHAPTER 1

What are they?

The sense of attraction, the purpose of love, the significance of anger or disgust, how we interpret our immediate surroundings, and how we express ourselves boil down to our basic feelings. Our emotions make most of our experiences unforgettable, either in a good or bad way.

Emotions are a sense of intense or mild feelings targeted at someone or something. On the other hand, emotion refers to states that are not geared towards something (as in anxiety and depression).

There are many different kinds of emotions that affect how we live and connect with others. At times, it might seem like these feelings govern us. The expectations we have, the decisions we make, and the actions we take are all predetermined by what we feel (our emotions). There have been attempts to classify the various emotions that people feel.

To categorize and describe people's feelings, scientists categorized emotions into two distinct classes: Basic and Combined Emotions.

Basic Emotions

A psychologist, Paul Eckman, defined this group. He described six basic emotions uniformly experienced in all human societies: happiness, surprise, anger, fear, sadness, and disgust. He eventually extended his list of real feelings to include shame, pride, embarrassment, and guilt.

Let's look at some of the fundamental forms of emotions more closely and discuss their effect on human actions.

Happiness

Of all the various kinds of feelings, happiness tends to be what people aspire to the most. Happiness is also characterized by feelings of contentment, pleasure, gratification, fulfillment, and well-being as a good emotional state.

Within various fields, including psychology known as positive psychology, research on happiness has risen dramatically since the 1960s. Often, this form of emotion is conveyed through:

- Body gesture: such as a gentle posture
- Facial expressions: such as gleaming
- Voice tone: an upbeat, delightful way of speaking

Although happiness is considered one of the raw human emotions, society appears to be highly influenced by the things we believe would produce happiness. Pop culture factors, for instance, tend to stress that satisfaction can result from achieving things such as owning a home or getting a high-paying career.

The truth of what leads to happiness is always much more nuanced and highly individualized. It's a general notion that happiness is intertwined with wellbeing, and it has also been postulated that happiness can enhance both mental and physical wellbeing.

Happiness is associated with several effects, including improved survival and enhanced marital satisfaction. In comparison, unhappiness is connected to a lot of damaging health effects.

Sadness

Sadness is another form of emotion often associated with feelings of dissatisfaction, grief, sorrow, unconcern, and mood dampening as a briefly expressed emotional state.

Like other emotions, sadness is something that all individuals encounter from time to time. People will experience severe and prolonged periods of sadness in certain situations, resulting in depression. It is possible to express sorrow in a variety of ways, including:

- Crying
- Dampened mood
- Lethargy
- Quietness
- Withdrawal from others

Depending on the root cause, the form and magnitude of sadness can vary, and how individuals deal with such feelings can also differ. Sadness may also cause individuals to partake in coping strategies such as avoiding other individuals, self-medicating, and ruminating on depressive thoughts. In reality, such actions may intensify feelings of sadness and extend the emotion's length.

Anger

Anger may be an emotion characterized by feelings of aggression, irritation, annoyance, and antagonism towards others that are especially strong. Like fear, rage can play a part in your body's fight or flight response.

You can be inclined to fend off the risk and defend yourself if a threat creates feelings of frustration. Anger (Rage) is expressed as:

- Physical expression: such as taking a strong stance or turning away
- Facial expressions: such as frowning or glaring
- Physiological reactions: such as face turning red
- The tone of voice: such as shouting

While anger is likened to a negative emotion, it can sometimes be positive. In a partnership, it can be constructive in explaining your desires, and it can also inspire you to take action and find answers to problems that concern you.

This form of emotion can have mental as well as physical effects. Unchecked rage can make sound choices challenging to make and can also impact your physical health. Coronary heart disorders and diabetes have been associated with anger. It has also been related to aggressive driving, alcohol consumption, and smoking that pose health risks.

Fear

Fear is a strong emotion that can also play a significant role in survival. You go through what's known as the fight or flight reaction when you encounter some form of danger and feel fear.

Your muscles are tight, your heart rate and breathing are increasing, and your mind is becoming more alert, training your body to either run away from danger or to stand and fight.

This reaction helps ensure that you can effectively handle risks in your world. Expressions of the emotion of this sort can include:

- Facial expressions: such as dilating the eyes and pulling back the chin
- Physical gesture: effort to hide or flee from the threat
- Physiological reactions: such as brisk breathing and heartbeat

Not everyone feels fear in the same way, of course. Some people may be more susceptible to fear, and this emotion may be more likely to be caused by unavoidable circumstances or objects.

The emotional response to an imminent threat is fear. We may also produce a similar reaction to anticipated threats or even our thoughts on possible hazards, which we usually think of as anxiety. For instance, social anxiety includes an expected fear of social situations.

On the other hand, some people seek out fear-provoking scenarios. It can be fear-inducing for extreme sports and other thrills, but specific individuals seem to flourish and even enjoy those feelings.

Surprise

Surprise is another one of Eckman's originally defined six primary forms of human emotions. Surprise is typically very short and is characterized after something unexpected by a physiological surprise reaction.

For instance, a surprise might involve someone jumping out from behind a tree and frightening you as you walk at night to your car. Surprise is often depicted by:

- Facial expressions: such as broadening the eyes and raising brows
- Body language: such as trying to hide or flee
- Verbal reactions: such as yelling, screaming, or gasping

Surprise is another emotion that can activate the sense of fleeing or fighting. The adrenaline rush that happens due to being startled or surprised prepares the body for flee or fight response. Surprise may have substantial consequences for human behavior. Research has shown, for instance, that individuals appear to note surprising occurrences excessively.

This is why in the press, shocking and rare incidents stand out. Studies have also found that individuals appear to be more motivated by surprising arguments and learn more from incredible results.

Disgust

Disgust is another of the original six raw feelings that Eckman mentioned. You can express hate in a variety of ways, including:

- Body language: repulsing the thing of disgust
- Facial expressions: such as rumple on the nose and twisting the lip
- Physical gesture: such as puking or retching

This sense of disgust, including a horrible taste, sight, or smell, may emanate from several things. Researchers suggest this emotion has developed as a response to foods that may be dangerous or fatal. For example, when individuals smell or taste foods that have gone wrong, disgust is a common reaction.

Bad hygiene, illness, blood, rot, and death can also cause disgust. This may be how the body stops stuff that can hold transmittable diseases.

When you witness others engaged in actions that they find distasteful, unethical, or wrong, you may also feel moral disgust.

Combined Emotions

It is possible to combine emotions to form different feelings, just as colors can be connected to produce other shades. According to this theory, the more fundamental emotions behave like building blocks. Mixtures of these more fundamental ones are more complex, often mixed emotions. Simple emotions such as joy and confidence can, for instance, are combined to create love.

The six raw feelings that Eckman mentions are only a fraction of different sorts of emotions that people can experience. Eckman's theory suggests that these central emotions are universal across cultures worldwide. However, the many different feelings and how they are categorized continue to be discussed by other hypotheses and new studies. Eckman later added several other emotions to his list but indicated that not all these could be encoded by facial expressions, unlike his original six emotions. Some of the feelings he described later included:

- Amusement
- Contempt
- Contentment
- Embarrassment
- Excitement
- Guilt
- Pride in achievement
- Relief
- Satisfaction
- Shame

Although, not all theorists agree on defining emotions or what the raw emotions are, as with many psychology principles. However, one of the best known is Eckman's theory. Other theories have suggested their ideas about what emotions form the center of human experience.

For instance, some scholars have proposed that only two or three raw emotions exist. Others also indicated that in something of a hierarchy, feelings exist. Primary feelings can then be further broken down into secondary emotions, such as affection, excitement, surprise, rage, and sadness. For instance, love consists of secondary feelings, including respect and longing.

These secondary feelings may then be further broken down into what are known as tertiary emotions. Tertiary feelings, such as liking, care, sympathy, and tenderness, contain the secondary emotion of affection.

CHAPTER 2

Destructive and Constructive Emotions

Our feelings grow on a timeline that begins with a stimulus that initiates the emotional experience and eventually leads to a reaction. In a sense, determined by our conditions and emotions, the event itself, and our worldview, the cause happens. Different responses will result from the same stimulus.

We might suppress feelings of anger at work, for instance, but demonstrate our frustration by yelling at a family member at home. Emotion denial can produce a short-term win, like preventing an argument, but if you are harmed by not standing up for yourself, it can become harmful.

"Whatever is begun in anger, ends in shame."

— Benjamin Franklin

Not all feelings are equal; they have different shapes and intensities. Annoyance, for example, is a mild expression of rage, while fury is the most intense form of the same feeling.

Our emotional experience clouds our understanding of a situation that filters through our feelings, people, and events. Your answer can turn emotion into a destructive one. Emotions are an indicator that they can escape danger or get you into trouble.

Our response is the last part of the emotional timeline and the most important one. Although regulating our emotions is not always easy, some reactions are more destructive than others. We must learn to understand our feelings instead of responding to them.

"In the past, compassion was something of a sign of weakness, or anger a sign of power, a sign of strength. Basic human nature is more compassionate. That's the real basis of our hope."

— Dalai Lama

According to Daniel Goldman, destructive feelings refer to an emotion that can lead us, either mentally or physically, to harm ourselves and others. Although the most common ones are anger, paralyzing fear, and depression, almost any emotion can cause harm. Craving and addiction can become harmful, even an unhealthy quest for happiness.

Emotions distort our ability to think clearly, making choosing the correct answer more complicated. When a destructive emotion occurs, we don't let new knowledge reach our minds in a refractory time, and we keep rehashing one specific emotion. Time and distance allow us to acquire clarity and make better decisions.

Take the example of a colleague who always comes to a meeting late. You do think that s/he insults you knowingly and interprets all s/he does as a personal assault. Our mind is trained by therapy, mindfulness, and meditation to shorten the refractory period. We learn to reflect instead of being blinded by our feelings.

By boosting self-awareness, we learn to wait before we react and choose a constructive response.

Destructive Emotions: Its Antidote

Scientists have realized that recurring negative feelings can cause long-term harm. This is the case for individuals suffering from cynical animosity, a trend characterized by elevated rage and frequent thoughts that others cannot trust. Individuals with pessimistic hate tend to get more cardiovascular disorders and also die at younger ages.

A constructive emotion is an antidote to a destructive feeling.

We must learn compassion, love, and patience to fight rage, hate, and fear. Destructive feelings, based on misconceptions and illogical motives, are impulsive. They are based on valid observation and reasoning. Constructive emotions are sensible.

"A calm mind directly leads to peace of mind"

— Dalai Lama

The consequence of constructive emotions is a relaxed mind that we see more vividly and realistically and understand life. What does an open mind destroy? Fear, distrust, hate, wrath, covetousness, and too much ambition.

"Just as we teach about physical hygiene in the interest of good health, we now need to teach about emotional hygiene."

— Dalai Lama

The Dalai Lama coined the word Emotional Hygiene to inspire us to take control of anger, frustration, and anxiety. Evil thoughts cloud our minds.

We've got to wash them away. The spiritual leader insists that we need to develop constructive ones as well, in addition to controlling negative emotions. Though they might not be useful in the heat of the moment, positive emotions help form a firm footing. They strengthen your 'emotional immune system.'

How to identify Constructive and Destructive emotions

Connecting how you feel is an easy way to understand this concept. Constructive emotions make us feel good, and destructive emotions make us feel bad or worse at some point. More importantly, constructive emotions help change a situation, and a problem appears to be made worse by destructive emotions.

Let's look at humor, for instance. Humor encourages us to feel comfortable and gives a funny joke to laugh at. Although if someone is the center of that joke, it may hurt that person. Grief and sadness can also be healthy, and help us in times of need to get support from others, making us vulnerable, which is okay. However, it can lead to depression if we let it linger, thereby becoming a destructive emotion.

It's that straightforward. Emotions are a crucial part of life as at some point in your life, you will experience emotions either constructively or destructively. Understanding what triggers these emotions and why you feel them can go a long way toward helping you feel better and improving your situation.

CHAPTER 3

How to deal with emotions – Learn to self-monitor

Self-monitoring involves self-awareness and management of self. Or more specifically, it consists of learning to recognize your emotions when they're emerging and developing the skills to manage this emotional state. Managing your emotions in details include:

1. Recognize emotions

Take the time to step back and observe your thoughts. How're you feeling? What are you going to experience? Naming our feelings is the first step towards raising consciousness.

Some people confuse rage with fear and learn how to discriminate against their emotions. Get acquainted with how each feeling manifests. The post below will help you dig into each emotion more deeply.

2. Know the triggers

Comprehend what sets you off. Recognize the signs or triggers that your decision will cloud. Is there some unique event, context, or individual that causes typically harmful emotions?

To focus on your emotions, review recent events and use the Emotional Timeline. What did you learn? What would you do better next time? Why?

3. Connect with your body

The only way we express our thoughts is not through our facial language. Recognize how your emotions influence your body. Note changes in your breathing rhythm, body temperature, heart rate, muscle knots, sensitivity to the skin, etc.

Our body is an incredible emotional conductor. Heed your reactions and physical well-being. Learn to avoid tensions or avoid harming your body by making room before you act. Do not allow emotions to create harmful patterns.

4. Manage your reactions

Do you focus on how you generally react to a particular situation? Before you answer, learn to pause. Emotions typically produce a rapid impulse to respond; we make space to think before our emotions hijack our actions by training our minds.

5. Adjust and learn

Emotional Hygiene involves learning to interpret, appraise and communicate our emotions correctly. In addition to enhancing well-being and social relationships, the emotion-management ability also helps resolve restricting habits such as procrastination.

Training the mind is not a straightforward path that needs constant practice and modification. Learn to deal with the rage if you feel frustrated. To behave more skillfully, you need to let go of the emotion.

Training can enhance your ability, but when you get back to overreacting mode, don't get frustrated. Be gentle with yourself and be kind. For loving-kindness, compassion, and happiness, a clean mind creates space. The antidote to negative feelings is emotional hygiene.

Now that we have established the types of emotions there, how do you recognize these emotions when they surface? How would you be able to identify them? These questions and their straight answers are core determinants in our journey of building emotional resilience or bouncing back.

Human emotions have morphed so that we can react to life-or-death situations faster. After all, while fear can stop us from acting in a 'life-limiting' manner, frustration can lead us to protect ourselves or those closest to us.

While proof suggests that certain emotions are universal, there is no one-size-fits-all emotional balance that suits every person's culture. We should stay cautious and avoid seeing clients who need to be fixed and may differ emotionally from ourselves. Nevertheless, we all benefit from a better understanding of our feelings and how they affect our actions, mainly when they are at odds with our daily and lifelong objectives.

However, there are many ways to help someone gain insight into their feelings, most of which start by identifying and recognizing them before exploring how they feel, think, and behave:

- **Recognize emotional thoughts**

Emotions may be recognized by their impact on our cognition (Peters, 2016):

- Irrational – making rash decisions without due considerations of possible reasons
- Emotive judgment – conclusions made quickly, based on feelings rather than facts
- Jumping to an opinion – triggers that make you concluding without all the necessary information
- Double-sided thinking – at times, we can be stringent, and we ignore the shades of truth or little pointers
- Escalating – overreaction enhanced by fierce emotion
- Delusional thinking – when we feel susceptible, we often become delusional

- **Self-compassion**

We often harshly judge ourselves and others. And yet, much of what we go through is natural and experienced by everyone through positive and negative emotions. Mindfully practicing self-compassion can help you explore and engage with deeply held feelings, memories, and experiences while treating yourself with kindness (Shapiro, 2020).

Perform the following steps (either within a session or at home):

- Bring to mind one challenge that you would like to focus on, perhaps at work or at home.
- Write the situation down as objectively as you can.
- Mindfully (with interest and openness) identify any emotions or bodily feelings that arise without connecting with them.

Alongside each, write down supportive, compassionate statements you could say to yourself or a friend, for example:

- It's okay to feel this way.
- I am here for you.
- We all make mistakes.
- Reflect that it is natural to feel upset, lonely, frustrated, and fearful at times.
- Consider others around the world who may be going through the same thing.
- Show compassion to yourself and others in this or similar situations.

- **Talk about your feelings**

Talking about your feelings is very crucial in reviving your control sense, providing your perspective, and also subjugating stress triggers. Discussing issues out loud with a friend, family member, therapist, or even when alone not only allows us to see things differently, it also gives us time and focus to use logic and point of view, leading to:

- Reduced feelings of threat and anxiety
- Rationalized events
- Normalized emotions. We recognize that our feelings are normal and faced by others.
- Conversation like this can carry so much emotional weight, combining them with other activities can help (for example, taking a stroll, preparing a meal, etc.)

- **Reflection and reappraisal**

Throughout the day, while we each have many feelings, often passing by without much consideration, revisiting them can be helpful.

After all, it is vital to understand their emotions and whether their responses to events are logical or emotional if customers want to implement changes in their lives. Please ask them to:

Review some of the situations faced during the day.

Consider how they handled them:

- Was your behavior, or your response, based on emotional or logical thinking?
- Could you have dealt with the situation better?
- Now try putting yourself in someone else's shoes. How would they think you reacted?
- Time spent reflecting can help you recognize emotions, their effect, and future improvements.

CHAPTER 4

Expressing Your Emotions

"I was angry with my friend: I told my wrath, my wrath did end. I was angry with my foe: I told it not; my wrath did grow."

—William Blake, A Poison Tree.

Feelings and emotions can be healthfully expressed in four significant ways:

Athletically: In all stretching, fitness lessons, swimming, cycling, hiking, biking, weight lifting, and all kinds of sports, you can athletically express yourself, everything from baseball and football to soccer and basketball, tennis racquetball, track and golf, and many others.

Interpersonally: In-person, face-to-face conversations with others, couples, and family gatherings, telephone conversations, e-mail, and "snail" mail, writing in your diary or journal, community activities, engaging in a joint social movement with a friend or parent, counseling or coaching, and gathering support from co-workers and acquaintances may be conveyed interpersonally. Note, no part of a discussion about how you feel requires the term you are. Essential skills to develop and ideal for healthy emotional speech is giving voice, finding a voice, and speaking up for another.

Artistically: You can express yourself artistically through painting, pottery, video making, music, flower gardening or arrangement, video games, graphics, and general arts.

<u>**Spiritually**</u>: Through praying and listening to the Divine, you can spiritually express yourself, letting the Divine speak through your voice, engaging in religious ceremonies and spiritual activities, scriptural study, affirmations, meditation, getting in touch with Spirit in nature, and immersing yourself in the Love and Light of the Beloved.

One of the most complicated ideas of our lifetime is simplified by the Wheel of Emotions. It can be challenging to define and verbalize what we feel when asked about feelings that we experience subconsciously. The Wheel of Emotions encourages us to do the same, which is the first step in resolving any challenging situation. The wheel of emotions helps to recognize and define feelings and benefits to reflect emotionally. It also assists in the study of online text and as a networking tool. By propelling them towards self-growth, it empowers individuals.

There are five components to how emotions affect our actions:

1. Recognition

This aspect only involves feeling emotions. The individual watches how a particular series of events influence their internal universe and understands what they are experiencing.

2. Action

The body gears up to function once the emotion is identified. Not all of our conduct is affected by thoughts, and we can regulate the ones that are. If public speaking, for instance, fills you with anxiety and anticipation, you can still face fear and give a presentation.

3. Appraisal

To ascertain the cause of said emotions, human beings will examine their feelings and track their environment. Then, their emotional answers can be changed accordingly. The individual is exercising this assessment component in the above example.

4. Expression

This is a function of communicativeness. In the form of facial expressions, movements, and body language, it includes our feelings' communication. On the individual scale, it is critical.

5. Physiology

The chemical changes in our body in response to emotions are referred to by this feature. For instance, when you blush, the rush of blood to the face, or when you feel rage, the increase in body temperature.

CHAPTER 5

Myths you've been told about Emotions and the Truths

Emotions can often be frustrating and daunting, and common misconceptions about feelings can make it worse. Some theories suggest that at all times, you should be in control of your emotions. Other approaches associate the reality of who you are with feelings.

While growing up, you may have learned that some feelings mean you are greedy, overreacting, or needy. Or you could have been told that you are too emotional and that you could control your emotions if you only tried harder.

Myths cause needless miseries and make it more challenging to handle painful feelings. Here are some common myths about emotions and the truth about them.

MYTH: Getting powerful emotions suggests that I am out of balance.

TRUTH: You can feel deep, and you can't be out of equilibrium. The out-of-control aspect comes not from the feeling but the action.

People often combine the two, worrying that strong emotions would lead to impulsive or self-destructive acts.

For example:

- You felt very angry and lashed out at someone, ruining a critical relationship.

- You felt really hurt and prematurely ended the relationship, but later regretted it.
- You have repeatedly texted an ex in the throes of grief about the end of the relationship.

The behavior in the above cases contributed to feeling out of control, not the emotion in itself.

You can feel deeply and not be out of reach. You can learn to separate strong feelings from the action so that you can react wisely to painful life situations instead of reacting irrationally.

MYTH: Changing my emotions is inaccurate or inauthentic.

TRUTH: As people, we all continuously encounter emotions that we aspire to improve. That's not to suggest we're not true to who we are.

For example, if you're afraid to fly but want to see your friends and family all over the world, you're going to work to strengthen the emotional response of fear.

You might be terrified of going to an interview, but you want a job and need it. You learn to reduce your anxiety to succeed to become your best self.

MYTH: My emotions tell my real reality.

TRUTH: Often, powerful emotions, rather than the event itself, are based on our perceptions of events.

It is therefore difficult, mainly if you are emotional or very sensitive, to put too much weight on your feelings. Some passionate individuals develop an identity through their senses. Or their intense feelings make them unique, relaxed, or, they think, better than others. But it's not easy to have a clear sense of self when the context relies on something as fluid as changing feelings.

MYTH: Some emotions are silly.

TRUTH: This is one of the widespread myths about emotions that can restrain you. It is a way of invalidating yourself and your own experience to assume that any emotion is dumb, especially the feelings that make you feel uncomfortable, such as guilt, depression, or fear.

You should bottle it up or push it down, for example, so that if you feel frustrated or upset about not being selected to lead a project at work, you look like a team player. If a potential romantic partner decides they don't want a third date, you could reassure yourself that it's not a big deal instead of feeling the pain of disappointment. You might be blaming yourself for feeling depressed or angry and hoping that you wouldn't be so bothered by these kinds of things.

MYTH: Some people understand what I feel more than I do.

TRUTH: You are, essentially, the final say. Only you will know how you feel, honestly.

And if you've been invalidated continuously, it may be easier to look for someone to tell you what you thought—being validated means that others have acknowledged the feelings as worthwhile, rather than ignoring, condemning, or rejecting them.

Sometimes, it is easier to rely on what others think about what you feel if you are uncertain about your feelings.

MYTH: To be imaginative, I need to be very emotional.

TRUTH: Intense emotions can inspire works of art of all kinds as well. But to have the discipline to see your innovative ventures through, you will need access to your intelligent mind, which is a mixture of emotion and rationality.

Without the logical or reasonable part of you onboard, your emotions can be great fodder for creative content, but it'll stop there. It would be almost difficult to complete the music, painting, or short tale on emotions alone.

MYTH: I'll never stop if I start crying.

TRUTH: Currently, ignoring sadness or anger doesn't make it go away. It's still there in that sense, pulling you down. Many people struggle to feel their sorrow or disappointment and do anything to avoid suffering. The trick to experiencing feelings you think about is experiencing them in small doses, so you don't feel like drowning in painful emotions will overwhelm you.

MYTH: Emotions happen for no cause.

TRUTH: For emotions, there is always a cause. Even if the explanation isn't known to you.

Imagine, for instance, that all of a sudden, you feel sad when standing in a shop smelling a vanilla-scented candle. You just want to go home now. That's because the fragrance inspired an appreciation of the home of your grandmother that smelled of vanilla. She probably liked to bake memories and past associations that often occur outside of conscious perception, leading to the impression that you experience something for no reason.

MYTH: Being logical is better than being emotional.

TRUTH: We need our emotions! They make us respond rapidly in the face of danger, help those in need, and encourage us to form close relationships.

Ask yourself, if you had no feelings, what the world will look like:

Would you calm a crying baby?

Would you flee from a dog?

Would you have any friends?

Typically, when people say that it is easier to be rational than to be emotional, what people mean is that they don't trust their emotions not to get them into trouble. They may have had the experience of being so enthusiastic that all meaning went out the window. Once again, we need a mixture of rationality and emotion to be our most rewarding selves.

MYTH: My emotions depict who I am

TRUTH: Each human being is so much more than their feelings, mainly when they are highly emotional or sensitive people.

Our feelings are always in flux, continuously shifting like the tide. It is not abnormal to feel more than one emotion at once. And often, these various emotions fuse. At the same time, for instance, you might feel angry and sad about the same thing. It can be hard to pin one down long enough to call it your identity. It contributes to a feeling of wavering forever, being unsure of who you are. Know, it's going to be hard to have a healthy sense of self if you feel like your feelings are yours.

Part II

Understanding Emotional Resilience

CHAPTER 6

What is Emotional Resilience?

The capacity to adjust to difficult circumstances and deal with life's ups and downs is emotional resilience. Strength does not remove tension or eradicate the challenges of life; it helps you resolve or embrace issues, survive through hardship, and move on with life.

Although resilient individuals do not allow hardship to define them or their lives and can roll with the punches, they can succumb to stress, life changes, and more challenging situations. Being rigidly 'solid' can be unhelpful without versatility, leading to stress fractures.' In a storm, a resilient person is more like bamboo, bending rather than cracking, flexible and adaptable rather than rigidly resistant.

Emotional resilience is the capacity to produce positive feelings and rebound rapidly from negative emotional experiences. Despite stress and adversity, theorists define strength as the ability to show positive adaptation, and this aspect represents positive dynamic adaptation. Good feelings after challenges are supposed to be based on the following:

(a) undo the effects of negative emotions and speed cardiovascular recovery from a challenge.
(b) promote long-term resources.

Emotional resilience can see you through the darkest hours, but it doesn't just happen because you like it. Building up emotional strength takes some time and effort.

Emotional resilience can mean different things to different people in different situations. Take, for instance, someone just diagnosed with an illness that might cost their lives; for such a person, emotional resilience would be trying to remain mentally balanced to get the best out of the time they have to live while they can. Conversely, emotional resilience to a soldier at the war front, with their lives frequently at risk, is to try as much as possible to remain under control to keep them and their family safe.

Dr. Ben Weinstein, an American Psychologist, suggests that, in too trying times, the most common reaction of those directly affected is emotional resilience. In most cases, with time, such people heal on their own. Most people reading this book would not encounter disaster on a large scale.

Nonetheless, we all are susceptible to stressors and trauma at some point in our lifetime. It doesn't have to involve surviving a war or a terrible natural disaster. At some point, every one of us has come face to face with challenges that stirred up our emotional resilience - for instance, the trauma caused by losing a loved one. The person closely related to that friend or family member would be pushed to experience intense feelings of depression, guilt, and frequently, significant stress.

Likewise, in a case of being diagnosed with a severe illness or in problems such as criticism, disappointments, and setbacks at your place of work, undermining your self-confidence and ability to be better, provoking an array of negative emotions. These scenarios put out the ability to bounce back and regain control in our lives to the test.

And the complicated part is that, for some of us, our sense of self or self-worth and ability to regain control is bound to our material status. We tend to use temporal indicators like the size of the house we live in, the type of car we are driving, and the kind of money we earn to judge our success level (compared to others). The estimate of these indicators helps us find our sense of worth or purpose and determine how we see ourselves. As a result of this standard or accomplishment we have set for ourselves, a significant mishap in just one of these estimators can weaken our confidence and reduce our sense of worth of who we are and the value we are adding to people, whether at home or work.

By default, the comparison is the standard measure of accomplishment and growth, but it is not necessarily a healthy one. Author of one of the bestselling books 'The 7 Habits of Highly Effective People", Steven Covey puts it in the best way possible. He said, "Have you ever seen an unhappy horse or an unhappy bird? This is because birds and horses are always happy. After all, they aren't trying to impress other birds and horses, neither are they comparing themselves with others".

Having said this, being emotionally resilient means you show less sense of envy. Don't get it wrong though, being emotionally resilient doesn't mean you have to be unemotional or undesiring of the good things of life. Instead, it means that you can fully harness the power of emotions while being entirely immune to negative emotions.

If you have managed to evade comparing yourself with other people, that's very good. However, you aren't out of the ruffles yet—your sense of self-worth and level of self-esteem can be much dependent on the level of association or relationship with others. A setback in this aspect can also have severe implications for our ability to bounce back or recover. Dr. Gaithri Fernando, who is an expert in post-traumatic stress (especially stress as a result of severe trauma such as war), found out that after two to three years, many of the survivors of the Sri Lankan Tsunami had recuperated and incorporated their traumatic experience into their new life. However, Dr. Fernando suspected that this recovery might not be equal as survivors who lost their families could not move on. With puzzling questions like, "who is going to be their brother or sister now? Who would they be an uncle, father, son, or husband to now?

As we have seen, the level of emotional resilience varies per individual. Some people are better equipped to bounce back from life's turmoil and setbacks faster than others. Fully understanding why this is would require every individual to know their emotional resilience threshold. This would mean that there is a universal indicator for us to know our tipping point or the point where we can't go any longer.

Unfortunately, there is no universal indicator; we are all built differently and respond to circumstances and situations different from each other. Furthermore, an individual can be immensely resilient from a particular perspective but is weak from another perspective. For instance, someone who lost a child lost a close friend and got cheated on by their fiance handled all this swirling wind of mishaps well with family and close friends. Still, after a minor dispute or disapproval from a boss or colleague, they crumble and lose all sense of self-reliance. Like, they could handle all that grief just right, but a little dispute shatters their emotional shield.

Independently, we all have unique ways of reacting to situations and overwhelming events; that's a fact. The secret behind this is varying levels of self-awareness. Raising our self-awareness levels increases our chances of withstanding whatever events that may come our way. Understanding the sorts of events that can negatively affect us and then mentally tuning ourselves to be aware and ready for such events would reduce these events' impact on our emotional stability. At least, if an adverse event is inevitable, the need for it to be handled in the best way for a positive outcome to arise. It's normal to get faced with crazy situations, but we must bounce back quickly and come back strong.

Emotional Resilience embraces the fact that you're hurt and continues to grow along with the broken pieces. Not only can we respond to stress and disappointments when we are adaptive, but we also gain the wisdom to prevent behaviors that could lead us to face those circumstances. Consider the instance below:

Mr. Charles is a computer scientist, a responsible worker, a devoted husband, and a tremendous manager. Mr. Charles starts his work on time and concentrates. He is eager to learn from his mistakes, never postponing, and therefore, never misses a deadline or lets it escalate like many of his colleagues do. He is pleased with what he's been able to do so far.

We can deduce that Mr. Charles is emotionally resilient.

CHAPTER 7

Elements of Emotional Resilience

There are three building blocks of Emotional Resilience, which are the foundations on which we can create resilience or strive to strengthen it. The three dimensions of emotional stability are also known as:

1. The Physical Elements

Include physical strength, energy, good health, and vitality.

2. The Mental or Psychological Elements

Include aspects like adjustability, attention and focus, self-esteem, self-confidence, emotional awareness and regulation, self-expression, thinking, and reasoning abilities.

3. The Social Elements

Include interpersonal relationships (partner, work, kids, friends, community, etc.), group unity, likeability, communication, and co-operation.

Accepting that it is inseparably connected with other life forms is an essential part of creating emotional resilience. In your relationships, for example, building resilience at work will also make you resilient and vice versa. If the training is aimed at enhancing one specific area, it is bound to demonstrate its effect on other areas of life. Resilience development scheme aim at improving emotional resilience by building:

- **Self-Awareness**

The capacity to tap into our thoughts, inner tensions, and the world's interpretation is self-awareness. By gaining self-awareness, we gain a deeper understanding of how emotions relate to our behavior.

Instead of looking outside for help or blaming the world for our miseries, self-awareness gives us the strength to search inside ourselves for answers. Building self-awareness allows us to become more capable and intelligent by making us more attuned to our inner world.

- **Persistence**

Training in resilience helps a person cultivate the consistency and determination to keep trying. Whether coping with external stressors or managing internal disputes, the inner drive is kept alive by perseverance.

- **Emotional Control**

People with greater emotional and self-control levels would be able to redirect themselves and manage their emotions. They are less likely to be depressed or let it affect their lives through tension. Before taking the plunge, they deliberate and won't surge quickly into concluding.

- **Flexible Thinking**

In one of her Psychology Today publications, Alice Boyes stated that flexible thinking is an essential aspect of mental health that contributes to every human being's personal and professional success.

It is an excellent social skill involving optimism, adaptability, logic, and positive thinking. An individual who, through training or practice, has or has acquired these abilities will undoubtedly be more emotionally resilient and well-balanced in life.

- **Interpersonal Relationships**

It is both a by-product and a prerequisite for emotional resilience to have strong personal relationships. If we can develop good interpersonal relations at the professional or personal level for a resilient life, we have already taken one step forward.

In one of her articles, Jennie Phillips, Ph.D. in Social Sciences and Education at the University of Ontario stated that developing strong interpersonal relationships extends our vision, transforming how we see the world and ourselves.

Like Aristotle said, we are social beings, and being surrounded by individuals gives us the ability to conquer, survive, and grow from problems. We must have the ability to strengthen our current interpersonal relationships and be open to developing new ones to create emotional strength in a larger context.

CHAPTER 8

Developing Emotional Resilience

When we are faced with life's turmoil like a loss of a job, a severe sickness, partner infidelity, loss of a child, or loss of a profitable business opportunity or when we are beckoned to help a family friend or friend get through a particular turmoil or a sudden shift in their lives, it's normal for us to think that changing the circumstance surrounding the event or the condition can help calm the situation.

Even when we are taunted continuously with internal messages about how terrible we are handling the case, we still consider the possibility of fixing the external problem by bringing the solution and improve how we feel both on the outside and the inside.

Developing life skills, wisdom, and resources to orchestrate a change in the external circumstances we are faced with when possible and hold ourselves to withstand this situation when we can't. Invariably, that's what resilience is all about, right?

But what I would like us to understand is that focusing on what we are facing (the external problem) is every bit as important as focusing on what we are meeting on the inside. We must pay attention to the internal messages we are getting for every external stressor. We must pay attention to the internal messages we are getting regarding that event, about how well or how bad we are coping, especially in a case when the current event triggers memories of imminent danger from our past. And if we let what is happening to get the best of us, things can get worse quickly.

Our ability to be emotionally resilient, regain balance, find out the center, and keep going is determined by our wise and response capacity.

Whatever stuff could happen, the secret to dealing with the situation is how to manage it.

We change our perception/ attitude and our response/behavior. It might seem like external stressors, or negative internal signals on how we deal with them, have no end.

That's why the most successful option we can make to improve our resilience could be to create a change in perception (attitude) and our reactions to those stressors and those messages (behaviors). By refocusing your attention from what just happened to how you deal with what just happened, you will experience this power of changing your attitude and actions.

OMG! I dropped the vase! It's shattered into a dozen pieces. — that was my aunt's gift to me!

I'll call my aunt to tell her. Maybe we can get another special one — it would be an excellent reason to visit.

Four hundred bucks for new lights! That's huge!—And thank God it is fixable.

The doctor needs to carry out more tests. Not such good news. This is hard. Well, better to know, better to get the knowledge I need to deal with this head-on.

The main point of these examples is to help us understand how shifting our attitude and behavior in these circumstances can turn them in any case. Knowing this is a significant shift.

This transition is how we shift from "poor me" to an "I" motivated, engaged – A change from a fixed mindset to a mindset of growth, a way of holding the mind, being open to learning.

We can modify any internal signals that we can hear about how we have coped (or not) in the past or are coping (or not) presently. Strengthening resilience means seeing ourselves as individuals who can be adaptive, knowledgeable in managing, and skilled in learning to deal.

CHAPTER 9

The Human Brain Factor: Key to Building Emotional Resilience

You can grow and enhance emotional resilience because it is evolutionarily innate in your brain, reacting flexibly, deciding to choose wise actions, persevering in the face of doubt and discouragement. Our natural being is built to weather the heaviest of storms.

All your life, because of its neuroplasticity, your brain has the flexibility to establish new patterns of reaction to life events. A mature adult brain is physiologically intact, but it is flexible and versatile, not inert or fixed to function. Your brain will create new neurons, link these neurons to new circuits, incorporate new learning into recent memory and habit neural networks, and rewire those networks whenever it requires it.

The capacity of the adult brain to continue evolving and altering its lifelong functioning is, without doubt, the most exciting finding of modern neuroscience. About thirty years ago, neuroplasticity in the adult human brain was recognized as a scientific fact, with the advent of imaging technologies that enabled neuroscientists to see these changes occurring in the prefrontal cortex, the executive functioning core of the brain, as well as elsewhere in the brain. Neuroplasticity, at any step in the human life cycle, is the engine of all learning.

Neuroplasticity ensures that all the emotional resilience capabilities you need are recoverable and learnable. Even if your capacity to resilience in early life was not completely established, perhaps because of a lack of healthy role models, less than a stable early connection, or the experience of too many adversities or traumas before your brain developed the requisite circuitry to cope, you can now improve them. That is right. When old patterns no longer serve a positive function, the human brain can still learn new coping patterns, mount those patterns in new neural circuitry, and even rewire the old circuitry.

By your own decisions, by self-directed neuroplasticity, the neural networks that underlie your coping mechanisms and behaviors can be formed and changed. You can, you can. Now you can learn, change and develop, because your brain can learn, change and grow.

Some individuals appear more 'natural' resilient than others by biological and social factors, no doubt. Despite this, the good news is that anyone can take measures to achieve greater personal emotional resilience. Some helpful tips on building emotional strength are:

1. **Know boundaries**: There is a distinction between the source of your pain and you.
2. **Cultivate self-awareness:** Take time for your thoughts and your body to tune in. Label your emotions. Note when and why they are coming. Think of what is beneficial to you and what is unhelpful. Adopt what is useful and take care of yourself.
3. **Seek valuable connections**: Aim to be with people who are willing to listen and be compassionate and don't try to solve your problems or change you. Try to make people understand what you need and what you find unhelpful. Look for a business that makes you feel confident. Friends can play a role, family, tutors, a counselor, a helpline, or a related classroom, book, website, or training.
4. **Practice acceptance**: A part of life is tension, pain, and changes. Instead of repressing or denying it, it's more helpful to acknowledge the truth of pain. It's not about giving up; it's about accepting pain, realizing that it comes and goes and that you can live by taking care of yourself, doing what works, and allowing others to support you.
5. **Practice mindfulness:** Being without judgment or avoidance in the present moment is a powerful, ancient form of building healing and resilience. This requires extensive practice, but it's beneficial

when the results of gradually calling yourself to reality begin to manifest.

6. **Do not expect to get the answers instantly**: You have in-built abilities for healing. Trying to fix problems by force will prevent your natural equilibrium from being found, which could take time.

7. **Allow space for imperfection**: It is part of healthy living to make mistakes. Keep going, and by getting it wrong, don't get disheartened. Enable yourself not to do too many things at once and let go of those things that you don't have to do or that are not your duty.

8. **Allow others to be imperfect:** We are all fallible. If you are less critical and you embrace yourself, you will be more capable of extending this grace to others and encouraging them to develop it to you.

9. **Practice self-care**: Be aware of and seek out what you are nurturing and resources. Ensure you do not run empty. Healthy eating, getting adequate sleep, keeping good company, giving help and receiving help, have fun, relax, Exercising, and avoiding too much alcohol or stimulants nurture inner well-being.

10. **Consider and take realistic steps, your possibilities, and your goals:** Reflect on what is and what isn't in your power to change. The objective is to accept what cannot be altered and to consider what can be. Is there another way to see your present situation? Could that be in the future? What decisions do you have? What are your realistic objectives? To start with, these may be very small. Continue to go and don't give up.

11. **Just express yourself.** It can be beneficial to communicate things in words, to a friend, or creatively when things seem to turn around inside or you feel worried. By bringing yourself to the present, e.g., going to the gym, yoga, walking, photography, volunteering, baking, or practicing self-care or mindfulness, you may choose to free yourself from unhelpful ruminating.

12. **Retain things in perspective.** Try to look at day-to-day problems from a wider angle. It can also help to have humor, a sense of mission, caring and giving to others, and other spiritual perspectives.

13. **Trying to practice optimism.** Will a lousy scenario have a right side to it? Consider both sides, if so. If possible, allow yourself, even amid pain, to appreciate what is right. If possible, see disasters

as obstacles rather than insurmountable issues to be solved. Know and derive strength and trust from what you have overcome in the past and your previous successes.

14. **Note the signs of warning**. Note symptoms of weakness, such as sleeplessness, anxiety, hopelessness, joylessness, lack of appetite, headaches, or nausea, and then take care of yourself by talking to others and practicing self-care. Talk with your GP if warning signs continue.

15. **Nurture a good outlook on yourself.** Imagine that you're a best friend of your own or someone you care for. What kind of care, compassion, patience, kindness, hope, encouragement, and forgiveness will you give to this individual? Give yourself.

16. **Trust in yourself.** Attach less value to what others believe. Refrain from making parallels to others. Things are complicated, however. You are responsible for yourself, and you have options.

CHAPTER 10

Why Bother With Building Emotional Resilience?

As you move through your life, much of your resilience will build up spontaneously. If it doesn't, under the pressure of past traumas, you may begin to feel fragile, worn out from trying or weighed down. Anyone may benefit from having greater emotional strength, whether they're naturally resilient or not. Here are some of the reasons why your time and effort are well worth it.

- **Reduced susceptibility to illness as a Result of Stress**

You are less likely to become physically sick when you're emotionally resilient. Gastrointestinal disorders, heart disease, headaches, asthma, and diabetes are among the most common stress-related physical illnesses. Although stress may not (at least not the sole cause) be the cause of the condition, stress may make existing disorders and illnesses worse.

It is not the stressful scenario that triggers the issues, however. It's how you react to the stressor that makes the condition more likely to start or get worse and how well you bounce back. Then, having greater resilience will place you on the path to enhanced physical health.

- **Low Anxiety Tendency**

Anxiety comes as a stress response. How much healthier would it be if you could respond to your stressors healthily? When your resilience is strong, you prefer to take constructive steps to change your condition or solve the trauma or disaster of the past. You are more likely to set aside anxiety and concentrate on impacting the present situation. If you can do nothing outwardly about your case, if you have a high tolerance, you can change your thinking and approach to it. More quickly, you adapt, and anxiety decreases.

- **Decreased Depression**

You won't dwell on the negative aspects of hardship if your resilience is strong. Instead, you'll find ways to help you profit from your challenging situation. If there's no way out of it, you'll look for things you can benefit from the case, and when you can, you'll be more assertive about making adjustments. You do not get frustrated as quickly because instead of being trapped in depression, you adapt and move on.

- **Possibility of lifespan extension**

Relatively strong individuals tend to live longer than people who are not. In one study, individuals who felt a deep sense of mission lived seven years longer, on average. A significant resilience factor is a sense of intent. Ninety-two percent of the high-resilience adults thought their lives had meaning in a study of thousands of adults.

- **Lower Irrational tendency**

You're more likely to indulge in irrational or high-risk habits such as alcoholism, substance use, overeating, gambling, and placing yourself in physically risky conditions when you have low resilience.

Reason? Since you know no other way to deal with your problems, you can take these "easy ways out." Irrational habits generate more, not less, concerns. You feel less desperate because you are more resilient and are thus less likely to withdraw into risky practices.

- **Increased Work Presence**

Low resilience can help cause physical illness, depression, anxiety and contribute to high-risk behaviors, as already described. These can all take you away from work. Then you're not going to stop the effects of an illness, or you're not going to go because you're immobilized at home by the symptoms.

You could be very afraid of going back to that situation if your work environment is stressful. So, why not pick a more straightforward job? You can do that, but to go out and pursue the career and adapt to the new work environment, you would need enough resilience.

- **Enhanced Learning**

Kids under seven years of age are busy learning about themselves, their families, and their environment. Somehow, in their world, they know the basic facts about the things, people, and places well enough to work. How are they doing that? Most of them, since they have excellent natural toughness, can do it quickly.

You're more comfortable doing new things with greater resilience and discovering the world. Also, negative and mentally unhealthy thoughts don't cloud your reasoning. Even now, you can develop your strength and benefit from the enhanced capacity for learning that goes with it.

- **Better Family Interaction**

Isolation can seem like the best option when you're less resilient. You spend less time with family members who could assist you in several ways. You do not enjoy fun family moments or take part in family events. Teens also, by isolating themselves, struggle with their lack of resilience. In times of adversity, adults can choose that choice, too.

Family interaction just got better when resilience is in check. You get to enjoy quality time with your family and friends, gain from them and benefit from family resources.

- **Active Community Involvement**

At least some opportunities for fun, learning, volunteering, and making interpersonal connections are offered by every community. Only if you're out in the community can you take advantage of these benefits. You can contribute to community events and projects that positively impact you and others in the community with a high resilience level.

- **Better Work Results**

Being more frequently present and on time is just one aspect of work success. You also need to show good judgment, stay focused on the tasks required, and take the initiative to do more than is required. You're more optimistic and action-oriented with high resilience. Your mind is more precise than negative thoughts, enabling you to make sound judgments with the brainpower you need.

- **Improves Relationship Maintenance Ability**

When either or both of you have low endurance, it's tough to have a stable relationship.

If only one has high resilience over a long relationship, the partner may hold up the other. The partnership may suffer or have increased problems. You can feel taken advantage of if you're a high-resilience partner. You can enjoy supporting your partner through hard times, and in some situations, that's a positive thing. When it happens continuously, though, you may start to feel like you're more of a child than a parent.

If you are the one with the lowest resilience, life will not be easy for you. Contributing to the relationship and feeling like an equal partner might be difficult. You may become so dependent on your partner that you cannot work on your own if he or she is suddenly gone. You may not like the person you are becoming either. It is possible that this will cause your self-esteem to fall, and you might become mentally incapable.

Of course, at the moment, you or your partner may likely adjust to their situation. Courage can come at times in the unlikeliest ways. However, if you want a more precise route to resilience, it's best to take active measures to build it.

- **Life is not a Static place**

Right now, if your life is fair, and you've had a pretty easy life so far, you may feel like you don't need resilience. It's always been all right, and you don't think that things will change much. Although that might be valid at this very moment, a moment from now, you can never guess exactly what will happen.

Part III

Boosting the Resilience You Never Thought You Had

CHAPTER 11

A Step-By-Step Guide To Building Emotional Resilience

Step1: Build strong relationships and connections.

An essential part of building resilience includes being willing to accept a helping hand from the people around you. You may want to consider participating in groups or organizations in your area alongside the relationships you have with your family members and friends.

Being a part of your local community makes it easier to build a support network. Helping other people is another option. For both you and the individual you are helping, supporting others can be rewarding.

Step 2: Hold on to your perspective, despite adversity.

Things are often beyond your control when dealing with stressful situations or adversity. The one thing that you do have control over is how you view and respond to what's going on around you. Try thinking ahead to the future, even if you're stuck in the thick of it. Most likely, the situation you are in right now won't last forever, which means that things will eventually improve. Whenever you notice that you feel a little better, pay attention to that feeling and concentrate on it because it can give you the strength you need to keep going.

Step 3: Maintain focus

Try giving yourself attainable targets. Take at least one step per day that brings you closer to achieving those objectives. Do not cause you to be overwhelmed by the big picture. Alternatively, find one little thing that you can do every day to help you get where you want to go. All of those tiny acts add up and can give you a feeling of moving forward.

Step 4: Be active

Your first reaction could be to try and hide and wait for the issue when facing an uncomfortable or undesirable situation. However, a much safer way is to take action. It feels more comfortable to do anything to change the condition than to do nothing at all.

Step 5: Look for the silver lining.

The time you spend dealing with life's difficulties can teach you a lot about yourself. Anytime you are going through something challenging, you can learn more about your ability to handle adversity. Overcoming challenges can build your self-confidence. It can also help you develop more robust, more meaningful relationships and can increase your capacity for appreciation.

Step 6: Trust yourself.

Approach challenges with confidence, using your instincts to guide you. Each time you overcome something difficult, it can help you see yourself in a more positive light.

Step 7: Be realistic.

Try to see things from a broader viewpoint, even if you are struggling with something too challenging. When you are caught in the middle of them, problems that appear unmanageable are always less severe than they seem when you see the effect they can have on your life over a more extended period.

Step 8: Don't give up hope.

Try to remain optimistic, regardless of what is going on in your life at present. Try to take a more optimistic perspective instead of concentrating on wrong things, thinking about what you want rather than focusing on the things that bother you.

Step 9: Constantly practice self-care

You need to care for both your body and mind during tough times. Take a moment to unwind. Do stuff you love. Exercise daily. All these acts will go a long way to develop your physical and emotional endurance.

CHAPTER 12

Recovery: Post-trauma Emotional Resilience Building Practices

In the field of post-traumatic development, researchers suggest five practices to help a person bounce from dealing with and recovering from past traumatizing experiences to gaining strength and developing a more profound sense of meaning and intent for living.

1. Accepting Situation as it is

It is not fair, whatever has happened. It should never have happened, but it did. The first step of accepting what happened draws on all the traditions of conscious knowledge and compassionate acknowledgment of ourselves - both the event and our impressions and responses. I'm Alive! I'll be able to cope with this! Affirm that!

2. Look to Other People

When you feel insecure, other people will provide safe havens in person, in memory, in imagination, where you don't have to hold it together or take care of someone else. This gives you a break before you can deploy the tools you have used to return to your inner balance and start healing and coping.

People may also be assets, offering assistance in inspiration, practical service, and safety nets. Individuals will help you work through and work through any problem you face for as long as it takes.

3. Seeing only Possibilities and Positivity

The immediate, tangible result of practicing gratitude, generosity, empathy, compassion, joy, peacefulness, and contentedness is resilience: flexibility to the big picture and confidence. The clear, observable outcome of choosing to answer life's challenges from a growth mentality is persistence, striving to improve, and believing that you can learn. "Maintain a positive outlook" and "Instead of half-empty, see the glass half full" are not clichés. They are science-backed common sense wisdom.

4. Learn the Lessons

The brain begins to change how it perceives and reacts to the occurrence as soon as you try to "turn a regrettable moment into a teachable moment," as Jonah Lehrer says. Seeking the silver lining, finding the gift in error, is known to be the turning point in the post-traumatic development process. It is ultimately beneficial to learn the lessons in the case, not just to cope better in the future but to fare better at this present time.

5. Look at the Bigger Picture

You create a more vivid sense of the past, present, and future by putting a recent or potentially traumatizing occurrence in the broader context of your life. (One of the prefrontal cortex's integrative functions is the sense of continuity of the self over time.) You will start seeking a deeper understanding of meaning and intent for your life, not only despite the incident but also as a result of the experience. Your resilience starts to build a real sense of survival and progress.

When you can pull together the activities in this book to practice gratitude mindfully while walking with a friend in nature, calling on your caring friend to relieve the pain of every inner component, your resilience becomes almost unshakeable. You're going to be prepared to deal with anything and everything and to have confidence that you can cope.

Part IV

Gaining Resilience through Motivational Quotes and Mantras

CHAPTER 13

Motivational Quotes To help boost your Emotional Resilience

All of us have faced unique difficulties and stressors amid the pandemic. Although real economic, mental, and emotional challenges and no simple "fix" or escape from how we perceive our experience, it can make a huge difference.

Science teaches us, in truth, that what we tell ourselves in challenging moments matter. Even one negative word can activate the brain's fear center and impair our capacity to reason. On the opposite, inspiring or changing words or phrases from context will allow us to reframe and correct the path in real-time from stress.

Here are some mantras to help you stay optimistic and resilient in tough times.

1. "I don't break; I bend."

"The mantra, 'I don't break, I bend,' has helped me remain resilient throughout the last few months. This mantra reminds me that I am flexible, adaptable, and unshakeable in the face of adversity. When fear creeps in, I am reminded that I can handle it and not fall victim to it. When I'm having a bad day, I write this on a sticky note and stick it on my monitor to help keep me going."

—Alyssa Swantkoski, executive assistant, Denver, CO

2. "Clear on the outcomes, flexible on the approach."

"For the past fifteen years, I have lived by a simple but powerful mantra. During the pandemic, this mantra has resonated more than ever before. Everything from working to exercising to raising children has been upended. Staying focused on critical outcomes — for example, quarterly revenue goals, health benchmarks, and educational goals for children — is critical. You might not be able to approach your goals as you did in the past, but it doesn't mean you can't keep reaching and exceeding your goals. Shifting focus from uncertainty to outcomes is a great way to reclaim efficacy."

—Dr. Camille Preston, business psychology at AIM Leadership, Cambridge, MA

3. "Trust the process."

"My family members are all huge basketball fans. I am more of a casual basketball observer. Even though I am not a loyalist, I am a fan of the 76ers motto, 'Trust the process.' It has become my go-to affirmation during this time. Although there will continue to be uncertainty, I believe having patience, faith, hope, and trusting the process will help us grow and rebuild."

—Monique Johnson, nonprofit COO, Richmond, VA

4. "I am not alone in this."

"In these high-stress moments, I sometimes get momentarily lost in the personal challenges COVID-19 has created for me. In those moments, I try to shift my focus by repeating the following mantra: 'I am not alone in this.' I remind myself that there are so many others who are facing greater challenges through this pandemic. It gives me perspective and helps me feel grateful that I can manage my challenges."

—Marcia J. Hylton, corporate marketing strategist, El Paso, TX

5. "Warrior."

"My mantra that I like to repeat to myself is 'Warrior.' I keep telling myself that I am a warrior and I'm strong enough to face any adversity that comes my way. When anything happens, I ask myself: 'How would a warrior behave in this scenario?' It's a simple way of getting yourself into the right frame of mind to face any challenge!"

—Celia Gaze, managing director, Bolton, UK

6. "Live right. Be worthy. Make a difference."

"Resilience is a journey of grace and forgiveness — for myself and others. This phrase helps me feel grounded, hold myself accountable, reinforce my dedication to serving others, and know that we are all worthy of love. It's been my go-to mantra throughout this time."

—Elizabeth Blackney, activist, Williamsburg, VA

7. "Turn fear into fuel."

"I use this mantra as a reminder to myself that being scared is not a reason not to do something that could be productive, interesting, or put myself or my business in forwarding motion. And the bonus is that if it is something I need to say this about, then typically I am that much more proud of the accomplishment when it's done."

—Suzy Haber Wakefield, apparel design consultant, Montclair, NJ

8. "I am the hero of my own life."

"This is the title of a guided journal by Brianna Wiest, and repeating this mantra reminds me to always focus on what I can control rather than what I can't. It reminds me that nearly everything is in my hands and that I can choose to respond to whatever I'm faced with however I want. It also reminds me to demand the best for myself consistently: whether that's how I spend my time, the projects I say yes to, or the people I work with. It reminds me not to settle for the ordinary or to hold back when I know I have something worthwhile to contribute."

—Jodie Cook, social media agency owner, UK

9. "Small progress is still progress."

"Working in senior living and healthcare, this has been the mantra I've been living by during the pandemic. These are words of encouragement for those who have struggled. Our landscape has changed each day, often hour to hour, and everyone has brought something to the table to provide some hope and stability to our residents and families."

—Tamara White, training and education partner,
Kitchener, ON, Canada

10. "Breathe."

"Whenever I start feeling out of sorts, triggered, or anxious, I remind myself to breathe. I immediately start focusing on my breath, and with awareness, my breath automatically starts to change; it starts deepening and becomes fuller. This mantra is my reminder to expand on consciously deepening my breath. I stay in the moment, breathing in and out, which calms my body and mind and grounds me. It works every time."

—Donna Melanson, yoga teacher, Boca Raton, FL

11. "I have wisdom within."

"One phrase that I have found powerful during this time has been 'I have wisdom within.' This small mantra reminds me daily to slow down the mind chatter and tune into the knowledge base that exists in my bones. It has been so powerful that I have shared it with friends as a way to remind ourselves to tune in and listen, versus tune out and give our power away."

—Dr. Tricia Wolanin, clinical psychologist and community
wellness consultant, Bury St. Edmunds, UK

12. "You are already everything that you want to be."

"When I wake up in the morning, the first words that come out of my mouth are 'You are already everything that you want to be.' Most of us tend to want things from a place of lack, which only attracts more lack. Knowing and stating that I already have what I want takes desperation out of the equation. It always helps me reframe."

Manning L. Cromer

—Wemi Opakunle, author and coach, Los Angeles, CA

Other Relevant Quotes Are:

1. "Resiliency is something you do, more than something you have. . . You become highly resilient by continuously learning your best way of being yourself in your circumstance." — Al Siebert

2. "Resilience is overcoming adversity, while also potentially changing, or even dramatically transforming, (aspects of) that adversity." — Angie Hart, University of Brighton

3. "Resiliency is the ability to spring back from and successfully adapt to adversity." — Nan Henderson, author of Resiliency in Action: Practical Ideas for Overcoming Risks and Building Strengths in Youth, Families, and Communities.

4. "Resilience or hardiness is the ability to adapt to new circumstances when life presents the unpredictable."— Salvatore R. Maddi, Psychologist and author of Resilience at Work: How to Succeed No Matter What Life Throws at You

5. "Resilience isn't a single skill. It's a variety of skills and coping mechanisms. To bounce back from bumps in the road as well as failures, you should focus on emphasizing the positive."— Jean Chatzky, financial journalist and author of Money Rules: The Simple Path to Lifelong Security

6. "Resilience is knowing that you are the only one who has the power and the responsibility to pick yourself up."— Mary Holloway, Writer and Resilience Coach

7. "The strongest oak of the forest is not the one that is protected from the storm and hidden from the sun. It's the one that stands in the open where it is compelled to struggle for its existence against the winds and rains and the scorching sun." — Napoleon Hill (1883-1970), author of Think and Grow Rich

8. "Courage doesn't always roar. Sometimes courage is the quiet voice at the end of the day saying, "I will try again tomorrow."— Mary Anne Radmacher, author of Courage Doesn't Always Roar

9. "Courage is resistance to fear, mastery of fear, not absence of fear." —Mark Twain (1835-1910), humorist and writer

10. "Success is not final; failure is not fatal: it is the courage to continue that counts." —Winston Churchill (1874-1965), Prime Minister of the United Kingdom

11. "To be nobody but yourself in a world that's doing its best to make you somebody else is to fight the hardest battle you are ever going to fight. Never stop fighting." — e. e. cummings (1894-1962), poet, essayist, and playwright

12. "The last of human freedoms is one's ability to choose one's attitude in a given set of circumstances." —Viktor Frankl (1905-1997), psychiatrist, Holocaust survivor, and author of Man's Search for Meaning

13. "Resilient survivors handle their feelings well when hit with unexpected difficulties no matter how unfair. When hurt and distressed, they expect to eventually recover and find a way to have things turn out well." —Al Siebert

14. "During difficult times, an important resiliency step is being able to express your feelings in healthy ways. You can't make feelings go away, but you can move through them." —Al Siebert

15. "The better you become at being able to recognize, verbalize, and manage your feelings, the less you will be vulnerable to losing emotional control or developing cardiovascular illnesses."— Al Siebert

16. "Anyone who tries to act as though he or she never feels upset or distressed is more fragile than people who admit they need counseling."— Al Siebert

17. "Survivors are not afraid to have feelings. You must be in touch with your body and its messages." —Bernie Siegel, MD, author of Love, Medicine & Miracles

18. "When I dare to be powerful, to use my strength in the service of my vision, then it becomes less and less important whether I am afraid." — Audre Lorde (1934-1992), writer, feminist, and civil rights activist

19. "The truth will set you free, but first, it will piss you off." —Gloria Steinem, feminist, journalist, and social-political activist

20. "Cry if you want to, I won't tell you not to. I won't try to cheer you. I'll just be here if you want me to be." —Cole Porter (1891-1964), composer and songwriter

21. "I am down. And that is okay. I may be down for a while, but I will rise again. And when I rise, I will rise higher than I've gone before; I will be stronger than I've been before. I will thrive."— Brian Vaszily, author of The 9 Intense Experiences: An Action Plan to Change Your Life Forever

22. "Our greatest glory is not in never falling, but in rising every time, we fall." —Confucius, Ancient philosopher

23. "Fall seven times, stand up eight." —Japanese Proverb

24. "The truth is that falling hurts. The dare is to keep being brave and feel your way back up." —Brene Brown, shame and vulnerability researcher, and author of Rising Strong: How the Ability to Reset Transforms the Way We Live, Parent, and Lead

25. "I have always been delighted at the prospect of a new day, a fresh try, one more start, with perhaps a bit of magic waiting somewhere behind the morning."— B. Priestley (1894-1984), novelist, playwright, and broadcaster

26. "When you are hit with life-disrupting events, you will never be the same again. You either cope, or you crumble; you become better or bitter; you emerge stronger or weaker."— Al Siebert

27. "Things do not change; we change." —Henry David Thoreau (1817-1862), essayist, philosopher, abolitionist

28. "Change is inevitable – except a vending machine." —Robert Gallagher, editorial photographer

29. "If you don't like something, change it. If you can't change it, change your attitude." —Maya Angelou (1928-2014), poet, memoirist, and civil rights activist

30. "Never believe that a few caring people can't change the world. For, indeed, that's all who ever have."—Margaret Mead (1901-1978), author and anthropologist

31. "You must be the change you wish to see in the world." —Mohandas Gandhi (1869-1948), leader of the Indian independence movement against British

32. "The only way to make sense out of change is to plunge into it, move with it, and join the dance. —Alan Watts (1915-1973), philosopher, speaker, and interpreter of Eastern philosophy

33. "What most people call stress is an internal, physical feeling of anxiety or strain that they don't like. This is not just semantics. Stress is the external pressure; the strain is the internal effect." —Al Siebert

34. "It's not stress that kills us; it is our reaction to it. . . Adopting the right attitude can convert a negative stress into a positive one."— Hans Selye (1907-1982), endocrinologist and stress researcher

35. "Stress will break people altogether if they are at the beginning too weak to stand distressed, or else, if they are already strong enough to take the stress in the first place, that same stress, if they come through it, will strengthen them, temper them, and make them stronger."— Abraham Maslow (1908-1970), psychologist, creator of Maslow's hierarchy of need, and author of Toward a Psychology of Being

36. "The trouble with being in the rat race is that even if you win, you're still going to be a rat." —Lily Tomlin, comedian and actress

37. "Stress is nothing more than a socially acceptable form of mental illness." —Richard Carlson, psychotherapist, and author of Don't Sweat the Small Stuff . . . and It's All Small Stuff: Simple Ways to Keep the Little Things from Taking Over Your Life

38. "Blaming others for how bad things are for you keeps you in a non-resilient victim state in which you do not take resiliency actions." —Al Siebert

39. "The key to making your life better is to stop blaming others for triggering reactions in you that you don't like. The problem is not what others do; it is your reaction to what they do." —Al Siebert

40. "A Child Called It was a story about resilience; it was never about boo-hoo-hoo. It was about a kid that didn't quit."— Dave Pelzer, a survivor of extreme parental abuse and author of A Child Called It: One Child's Courage to Survive

41. "When we learn to deal directly with our complaints and difficulties, romanticized ideas about the spiritual path are no longer meaningful. We see that what is important is to take responsibility for ourselves, and always to be aware of our thoughts, feelings, and actions."— Tarthang Tulku, Tibetan teacher, and Buddhist

42. "Life is not a matter of holding good cards, but of playing a poor hand well." —Robert Louis Stevenson (1850-1894), author of Treasure Island, Kidnapped, and Strange Case of Dr. Jekyll and Mr. Hyde

43. "There are two ways of exerting one's strength: one is pushing down, the other is pulling up." —Booker T. Washington (1856-1915), educator and presidential advisor

44. "I didn't give up. I am not a victim, and that is my proudest accomplishment." —Suzanne Somers, actor and author of After the Fall: How I Picked Myself Up, Dusted Myself Off, and Started All Over Again

45. "You recover better when you tell your family, a friend, or a support group what you are feeling. If you'd like them just to listen and not problem solve while you talk, let them know. If you want some suggestions and coaching on what to do, let them know that". —Al Siebert

46. "Find a survivor who can be a role model for you. For me, it is Lassie: whenever I run into difficulties, I ask myself, "What would Lassie do now?" —Bernie Siegel, MD, author of Love, Medicine, and Miracles

47. "You all know that I have been sustained throughout my life by three saving graces – my family, my friends, and faith in the power of resilience and hope. These graces have carried me through difficult times, and they have brought more joy to the good times than I ever could have imagined."—Elizabeth Edwards (1949-2010), attorney and author of Resilience: Reflections on the Burdens and Gifts of Facing Life's Adversities

48. "Each friend represents a world in us, a world possibly not born until they arrive, and it is only by this meeting that a new world is born."—Anais Nin (1903-1977), diarist and novelist

49. "The bond that links your real family is not one of blood, but of respect and joy in each other's life. Rarely do members of one family grow up under the same roof."— Richard Bach, author of Jonathan Livingston Seagull and Illusions

50. "Nourishing relationships is the single most universally agreed-upon feature of the good life." —Daniel Goleman, author of Social Intelligence: The New Science of Human Relationships

51. "A few people are born resilient. The rest of us need to work consciously at developing our abilities." —Al Siebert

52. "Resilient children tend to have parents who are concerned with their children's education, who participate in that education, who direct their children's everyday task, and who are aware of their children's interests and goals."— Linda F. Winfield, author of Developing Resilience in Urban Youth

53. "Action is a great restorer and builder of confidence. Inaction is not only the result but the cause of fear. Perhaps the action you take will be successful; perhaps different actions or adjustments will have to follow. But any action is better than no action at all." —Norman Vincent Peale (1898-1993), minister and author of The Power of Positive Thinking

54. "Adversity reveals genius."— Horace, Roman poet

55. "Adversity introduces us to ourselves." —W. Mitchell, speaker, and author of It's Not What Happens to You–It's What You Do About It

56. "What does not kill me makes me stronger." —Friedrich Wilhelm Nietzsche (1844-1900), philosopher, poet, and Greek scholar

57. "A gem is not polished without rubbing, nor a person perfected without trials." —Chinese Proverb

58. "Every adversity, every failure, every heartache carries with it the seed of an equal or greater benefit."— Napoleon Hill (1883-1970), author of The Power of Positive Thinking

59. "Show me someone who has done something worthwhile, and I'll show you someone who has overcome adversity."— Lou Holtz, football player, coach, and analyst

60. "To succeed, people need a sense of self-efficacy, to struggle together with resilience to meet the inevitable obstacles and inequities of life."— Albert Bandura, psychologist

61. "It may sound strange, but setbacks make many champions."— Bob Richards, space entrepreneur

62. "Life is a succession of lessons which must be lived to be understood." —Ralph Waldo Emerson (1803-1882), essayist, lecturer, and poet

63. "Although the world is full of suffering, it is also full of the overcoming of it." —Helen Keller (1880-1969), deaf-blind author and political activist

64. "Strong people don't put others down. They lift them." — Michael P. Watson, professional boxer

65. "Our resilience increases as we recognize the magnitude of what we have already accomplished." —Patricia O'Gorman, author of Dancing Backwards In High Heels: How Women Master the Art of Resilience

66. "People are like stained-glass windows. They sparkle and shine when the sun is out, but when the darkness sets in, their beauty is revealed only if there is a light from within." —Elizabeth Kubler-Ross (1926-2004), psychiatrist, and author of On Death and Dying

67. "Empathy for other people's feelings requires a counter-balancing quality of toughness not to be controlled by their pain." —Al Siebert

68. "There are two ways of spreading light: to be the candle or the mirror that reflects it." —Edith Wharton (1862-1937), novelist and designer

69. "If I am not for me, who will be? If I am only for me, what is the point" —Hillel, fifth-century Jewish Leader

70. "Our primary purpose is to help others. And if you can't help them, at least don't hurt them." —Dalai Lama, Tibetan leader

71. "The most resilient people are like playful, curious children." —Al Siebert

72. "Taking time to laugh, appreciate pleasant moments, and smell the roses daily affects your brain and nervous system in ways that enhance your problem-solving skills, and this, in turn, increase your resiliency." —Al Siebert

73. "Joy in one's heart and some laughter on one's lips is a sign that the person down deep has a pretty good grasp of life." —Hugh Sidey (1927-2005), Life Magazine journalist

74. "Humor has bailed me out of more tight situations than I can think of. If you go with your instincts and keep your humor, creativity follows. With luck, success comes too." — Jimmy Buffett, musician, actor, and businessman

75. "Cracked up by life with a laugh that's known bitter but, past it, got better." —Jayne Relaford Brown, poet

76. "A person without a sense of humor is like a wagon without springs. Every pebble jolts it on the road." —Henry Ward Beecher (1813-1887), a clergyman and social reformer

77. "My life has been one great big joke, a dance that's walked, a song that's speaking. I laugh so hard I almost choke when I think about myself." —Maya Angelou (1928-2014), poet, memoirist, and civil rights activist

78. "Your mind and attitudes create either barriers or bridges to good outcomes."— Al Siebert

79. "Negative self-talk will weaken your self-concept and can lead to a self-fulfilling prophecy. People who think 'I'm a loser' or 'I'm a failure as a manager' tend to act in a way that confirms those beliefs. People who think 'I'm adaptable' or 'I'm a good friend' will tend to act in ways to confirm those beliefs". — Al Siebert

80. "The significant problems we face cannot be solved at the same level of thinking we were at when we created them." —Albert Einstein (1879-1955), theoretical physicist

81. "Wings are not only for birds; they are also for minds. Human potential stops at some point somewhere beyond infinity." — Toller Cranston (1949-2015), Olympic figure skater and painter.

82. "When one door of happiness closes, another opens; but often we look so long at the closed door that we do not see the one which has been opened for us." —Helen Keller (1880-1969), deaf-blind author and political activist

83. "I knew there was a way out. I knew there was another kind of life because I had read about it. I knew there were other places, and there was another way of being." — Oprah Winfrey, talk show host, actress, producer, and philanthropist

84. "The mind is its place and can make a heaven of hell and a hell of heaven." —John Milton (1608-1674), poet and man of letters

85. "Thinking is easy, acting difficult, and to put one's thoughts into action, the most difficult thing in the world." —Goethe, the ancient philosopher

86. "The person who is not hungry says that the coconut has a hard shell." —African Tribal Saying

CHAPTER 14

Mantras to Help Boost your Emotional Resilience

Science tells us that the way we talk to ourselves, especially during trying times, matters a great deal. In these moments, negative thoughts, self-doubt, and uncertainty can trigger our fear and impede our ability to reason.

On the other hand, empowering words and phrases can help you reframe your thoughts and shift your perspective to a more productive one. While positive thinking is centered around eliminating negative thinking, mantras and affirmations are more focused on building the mental muscle needed to manage challenges from a positive place.

"With emotional mastery, you have to give yourself cues. You have to give yourself affirmation. You have to tell yourself how to think, feel, and act." - Brendon Burchard

Much like we train our bodies and build our physical strength through exercise, we can train our minds to neutralize negative self-talk and rise above our internal dialogue. So here are some essential mantras that emotionally resilient people use.

—: Think of yourself as the hero of your own life -not the victim

Mantra: I am the hero of my own life.

Repeating this mantra will allow you to focus on what is within your control rather than what isn't. It's a reminder that you can choose how you react to what you're faced with.

Not only that, but it also keeps you accountable on your journey to be the best version of yourself. When you internalize this mantra, you're no longer subject to your negative self-talk, and you realize that you have a say in what's happening in your life.

Moreover, it teaches you that you're not a passive viewer and that you don't have to settle for less, especially when you know what you're capable of achieving.

—: Acknowledge that mistakes are part of learning -not proof of your shortcomings

Mantra: I have the power to pick myself up again.

Mistakes are inevitable, no matter how meticulous you are. The difference between emotionally resilient people and their counterparts is how they perceive these mistakes and what they take. Instead of considering this a failure on your part, choose to look at it as a learning opportunity. What matters the most is the knowledge and wisdom you gain from this experience, not how it makes you look to others.

—: Stay focused on your strengths

Mantra: I believe in my abilities, and I am committed to my purpose.

Believing in yourself is an essential part of building emotional resilience. So instead of dwelling on what you're not good at and what you can't do, focus on your strengths.

They're what make you unique and valuable. If you're having a hard time identifying your talents and abilities, you can ask a trusted friend or colleague. This may bring to light some qualities you didn't even consider in the first place. Self-understanding and self-support are fundamental in cultivating a better sense of fulfillment and progress. Challenge your negative self-talk, shift your perspective, and course-correct whenever you can.

This is key to developing greater emotional resilience. Not every day will be great, but learn to trust yourself and realize that little progress is still progress! Repeat these words of encouragement regularly to yourself, and you will witness a change in the way you tackle difficulties.

CHAPTER 15

Lifestyles That Can Help Boost Your Emotional Resilience

For your long-term health and well-being, preserving and nurturing the functioning of your brain is critical. You should make lifestyle decisions that secure, exercise, and improve the physical brain, which, in turn, supports the sophistication of all of your emotional resilience-supporting mental, relational, and cognitive functioning.

These following functions are healthy eats of life to enhance our emotional resilience-building ability;

- Pay attention to what you Eat
- Exercise and movement
- Sleep
- Learning something new
- Hanging out with healthy Minds
- Take a break from Gadgets
- Loosen Up More Often

The brain shift mechanisms that you use to get the most value for your brain are always coordinated through all the exercises: new conditioning, reconditioning, deconditioning at every degree of threat to your resilience. Start little by little, enjoy the entire process, and appreciate how the improved versatility and strength of your brain support your stability.

- **Pay attention to What you eat**

Without a doubt, you indeed are what you eat. All the nutrients our body and brain get comes from what we eat and drink. Researchers have identified foods that stimulate good brain health; The MIND diet (standing for Mediterranean Intervention for Neurodegenerative Delay) is an excellent example of such groups, proposed to help curb, decrease, and nullify cognitive damage aging. The MIND diet includes lots of vegetables, dark leafy greens, berries, nuts, beans, fish, whole grains, and poultry.

- **Exercise and Movements**

Vigorous exercise helps the brain release a neurotrophic factor secreted in the brain. This is the hormonal growth factor that causes new neurons to develop in your brain, especially in the hippocampus (the brain structure responsible for integrating learning into long-term memory from recent experiences).

These neurotrophic factors secreted in the brain also activate these new neurons to enhance their dendrites' length, density, and complexity, producing "thicker," more advanced brain networks. Furthermore, these neurotrophic factors speed up new neurons' maturation into fully functioning brain cells. This protects associated structures from brain atrophy and cognitive impairment, such as the prefrontal cortex.

Exercise makes you more knowledgeable. It will help you think well into old age, more clearly. As you age, exercise can also help overturn memory loss.

The adult brain only weighs about three pounds, but the brain uses only 20% of all the body's oxygen. Regular exercise helps the heart to pump more blood into the brain, increasing the brain's supply of oxygen and glucose that fuels all the activity of the brain.

Furthermore, exercise activates the release of essential neurotransmitters such as dopamine, serotonin, acetylcholine, and norepinephrine that activate different brain activity forms; endorphins make you feel better acetylcholine improves alertness. Exercise is a powerful antidepressant in head-to-head clinical trials due to these results.

Training regenerates our telomeres, the protective protein sheaths at the ends of our chromosomes, similar to the plastic caps at the ends of our shoelaces that prevent the unraveling of our shoelaces. Since telomeres avoid our chromosomes' unraveling when they replicate, preserving our telomeres protects our DNA from copying errors and increases our safe life span. With this, you should not be worried about terminal illnesses or system overdrive.

For the brain to produce feel-good endorphins, the body needs to move for about thirty minutes a day. Five days a week is terrific. It also applies little and often here: moderate exercise over many days is more productive (and safer) than a massive workout once a week.

Bilateral movements (moving the two sides of the body alternately, thereby activating the two hemispheres of the brain alternately) are behaviors such as running, brisk walking, bicycling, swimming, and using the stair climber at the gym.

They have an incredibly relaxing effect on your nervous system while nourishing your brain. Exercising with others, such as dance, tennis, basketball, and volleyball, stimulates the structure of social interaction, provides a sense of brain protection and primes its neuroplasticity.

In the lower brain, tasks such as these also engage the dopamine pathway of enjoyment and reward that keeps you motivated. To keep the workout routine fun, change it up. To extend your options and increase your motivation, invite a friend or attend a decent gym.

- **Sleep**

Enough sleep and deep sleep are essential to the well-being of the brain and body. Many of us don't get enough sleep routinely; our lives are too busy, too exhausted. In particular, young people don't get enough sleep.

At a stage of development where their brains need eight or nine hours to finish developing, teenagers will get five to six hours of sleep a night. Lack of sleep, particularly brain health, affects your metabolism, immune system, and genetic health, which in turn regards your ability to build an emotionally resilient persona.

You probably have the same level of cognitive impairment if you get just five or six hours of sleep every night for a week, as if you were legally intoxicated. When you are asleep, the brain is performing these essential tasks by doing "nothing":

1. Integrating learning and memories the day and stashing that knowledge in long-term memory. Sleep maximizes brain function, restores the ability to process data and quickly retrieve data while you are awake.

2. The restoration of the nervous system's balance. Sleep absorbs cortisol, a stress hormone. Sleep is the only time the brain is free of norepinephrine (adrenaline), without emotional charge, and processing memories of the day. As a result, by the time you wake In the morning, you feel less tension.

3. Standard brain cleansing. Dead and atrophied neurons are washed out.

4. Letting the prefrontal cortex relax and regulate the impulses from its executive activity, making it better able to function the next day again. You have also found that when you are tired, your judgment and impulse control is compromised.

- **Learning Something New**

All the time, the brain learns and rewires itself from experience. The more nuanced the experience or learning, the more complex the brain's processing since the new information is taken in and processed by more of our senses and regions of our brain. The function of integration and complexity that harnesses the brain's neuroplasticity is a defense against the loss of brain cells by brain atrophy as we age. It's called cognitive reserve construction. When you were younger, you did so by going to college or by learning a craft. You have more brain cells in the bank by keeping the brain healthy, so to speak, to prevent the brain cell loss that inevitably comes with aging.

- **Hanging out with healthy Minds**

Here we concentrate on the influence, casual and personal, of social interactions with individuals to promote brain health and psychological health. In social events, book clubs, choirs, bowling leagues, volunteer organizations, or political campaigns, you can already participate.

What might be new to you is distinguishing who has also established their relational intelligence abilities among the like-minded people in these groups and can participate in deep conversations with you from their safe interdependence. This is not true of all you meet all the time, of course, but it is well worth searching out such people.

When we mature and pass through life in new ways, we keep changing. We coevolve with others often, and marriages, friendships, business alliances, social organizations remain intact and thrive.

Shared interests and life paths often diverge, and we find ourselves drifting out of contact with individuals who once were close and essential to us. Perhaps we are no longer as accommodating as we once were to hang out with unhealthy minds in our own maturing and healing.

- **Take a break from gadgets**

At least 40% of waking time is spent on a digital device by an average American adult, every 6.5 minutes checking their mobile phones. On average, American teens spend 50 percent of their waking time on smartphones, and within five minutes of waking up, 25 percent of teens use a smartphone.

While generally accepted as natural, spending so much time on digital devices has significant implications for brain function and person-to-person relationships. Our minds are not machines, and it's not a replacement for face-to-face experiences to communicate with individuals via computers and phones. Researchers record our rapidly growing overuse of digital devices. The progressively adverse impacts on our brains, our relationships, and our resilience are recognized, particularly the effects on young, still growing brains.

One of the best things you can do with it in a world where your brain is continuously bombarded with texts, emails, tweets, and posts is to let it rest. Take a break, prolonged stretches of concentrated attention that consume resources and overstimulate incessant incoming messages that can adversely affect some of your brain's critical capacities.

- **Loosen Up More often**

Most people think of laughter as a feeling or something close to one. Oh. Not so. Laughter is a physiological process in the body and the brain that decreases stress. Laughter activates neurotransmitters that make the brain feel sharper and lighter, like catecholamines, dopamine, and norepinephrine. Laughter is also an excellent way to crack the ice and bond with individuals, and the brain is super good at bonding with individuals. Play gives the brain a good workout by meeting or developing new scenarios, falling into the default mode network in the brain, thinking up new rules, new characters, or new worlds. Play often also creates joy, a sense of interaction in our universe with other people or things, and a sense of relaxation and ease. All of these are also beneficial for the brain.

"Those who play rarely become brittle in the face of stress or lose the healing capacity for humor."

— STUART BROWN, Play: How It Shapes the Brain, Opens the Imagination and Invigorates the Soul

---

We may be so distracted and under strain that we forget to laugh and play, and then we forget to laugh and play. You could never have known how to safely laugh and play if you endured a lot of pain in your early life. With practice, this ability is entirely salvageable

Part V

You and Emotional Resilience

CHAPTER 16

Emotional Resilience: What It Is to You and the People around You

Demonstrating Resilience as an Individual

So what does it look like to demonstrate resilience? I have outlined several factors that contribute to and act as markers of strength, and they include:

- The desire to make concrete plans and take action to implement them.
- A positive opinion of yourself and faith in your skills and strengths.
- Communication and issue-solving skills.
- The ability to withstand intense sentiments and urges

Glenn Schiraldi (2017), author and resilience specialist, offers many more examples and attributes of resilient individuals, listing qualities, characteristics, and coping strategies that are strongly associated with resilience:

- Sense of self (having appropriate separation or independence from family dysfunction; being self-sufficient; being determined to be different perhaps leaving an abusive home; being self-protecting; having goals to build a better life)
- Tranquility under pressure (stability, the ability to regulate stress levels)

- Rational thought process
- Self-esteeming
- Optimism, Optimism
- Happiness and the intelligence of emotions
- Meaning and Goal (believing your life matters)
- The Humor
- Altruism, devotion, and compassion (learned helplessness),

Also, these characteristics are mentioned by Glenn Schiraldi:

- Character (integrity, moral strength)
- Curiosity (which is directly relevant to focus and interested involvement)
- Balance (engagement in a wide range of activities, such as hobbies, educational pursuits, jobs, social and cultural pastimes)
- Social functioning and maturity in society (getting along, using bonding skills, being willing to seek out and commit to relationships, enjoying interdependence)
- Adaptability (persistence, trust, and flexibility; recognition of what cannot be controlled; use of innovative abilities to solve problems and successful coping strategies)
- Religious inherent faith
- A lengthy viewpoint on suffering
- Healthy habits for wellbeing (getting sufficient sleep, nutrition, and exercise; not using alcohol or other substances immoderately; not using tobacco at all; maintaining good personal appearance and hygiene)

To sum up, if a person knows (both of themselves and the world around them), they effectively control their emotions, maintain a grip on their thoughts, feelings, and behaviors, and realize that life has its inevitable ups and downs.

CHAPTER 17

Additional Benefits of Being Emotional Resilient

For a good reason, you hear a lot about growing and improving resilience - both in ourselves and children. Joshua Miles, therapist, and counselor mentions a few of the large variety of factors why resilience is a valuable quality to have:

- Greater resilience contributes to better learning and academic performance.
- Resilience is linked to decreased absences due to illness from work or education.
- It contributes to reduced risk-taking behaviors, including excessive drinking, smoking, and the use of drugs.
- Those with greater resilience tend to engage more in family groups and events.
- A lower mortality rate and increased physical wellbeing are linked to higher resilience (2015).

The Effects of Emotional Resilience on Overall Health

While every point in that list is a good reason to pay attention to resilience, the last could be the most important. Resilience has a positive influence on our wellbeing (and vice versa, in some ways). A recent analysis of resilience studies showed that stability leads to or contributes to many different positive health outcomes, including:

- The experience of more positive feelings and more robust management of negative feelings
- Less depressive symptoms
- Greater stress tolerance
- Better dealing with stress by strengthened problem solving, constructive orientation, and stressor re-evaluation
- Despite age-related difficulties, good aging, and an enhanced sense of well-being
- Better recovery after an injury to the spinal cord
- Better symptom control of PTSD

Also, Harry Mills and Mark Dombeck, resilience experts, point to studies that resilience improves the immune system's functioning. Resilient individuals can handle negative feelings better and experience more positive emotions, leading to statistically good health results such as more immune system cells and increased immune function in cancer patients and more favorable mortality rates in marrow transplant patients.

As well as enhancing your physical wellbeing, optimistic thoughts improve your social health. Sharing positive emotions with others helps tie people together, build reliable, stable, and loving relationships, and sustain them. In exchange, loving relationships offer social support that nourishes more emotional resilience and positive feelings.

It is a trend towards wellbeing that is circular, self-reinforcing. The happier you feel, and the more you share that positive feeling with others, the more you can build on the connections that you create to create more positive emotions through that sharing.

The social support benefits of relationships are numerous and essential:

Relationships provide opportunities for expressing and receiving affection, both of which are important for identity, self-worth, and self-esteem. They provide a path to being part of something greater than yourself that you will remember in a meaningful way. They save you from feeling like you are lonely. You are down whenever you feel loved. They are settings in which optimistic states are likely to be experienced:

- feeling welcomed and cared for, and

- happy cheerfulness.

Communication, reciprocity, and kindness are encouraged by healthy relationships. They also act as a sounding board and can provide reality testing opportunities. Friends will offer workable solutions to concerns that you might never have come up with independently.

Relationships will support you economically (by helping you to find jobs or work opportunities) and romantically by giving you opportunities to network with people you would not otherwise meet (by introducing you to potential romantic partners).

Where positive feelings help you to create relationships, the reverse is achieved by negative feelings. Depressed states of negative emotion tend to break down relationships and erode social support. Destructive emotions tend to be consuming, and self-centeredness is encouraged.

They do not encourage individuals to attend to the needs of others. While friends and family frequently want to support their unhappy relationship partners, depressed, pessimistic individuals tend to withdraw from support offers and separate themselves.

Conclusion

There are real advantages of being resilient in terms of wellbeing and wellness. If you're not that way already, it's something worth working toward. Importantly, resilience is a learnable ability. If they work at it, most people will become more emotionally resilient.

Growing emotional resilience allows you to work for greater awareness of yourself. For example, you must learn to identify how you respond to emotional situations. It helps you gain more control over those reactions by being aware of how you respond when stressed. Emotional Intelligence is a helpful framework to help direct you to become more conscious of your feelings.

Overall, it can be described as your ability to use your emotions intelligently and appropriately in different circumstances. Emotionally smart individuals can correctly identify and understand emotions, both in themselves and in others, to communicate feelings adequately and to be able to regulate their own emotions to promote their mental, intellectual and spiritual development. In short, emotionally intelligent people use their thinking and actions purposefully to direct their feelings instead of letting their emotions control their thinking and behavior. People who are emotionally intelligent often appear to be highly resilient to emotions.

To become more emotionally intelligent, it is necessary to develop the following five skill domains:

Self-awareness: Self-awareness involves your proficiency to comprehend feelings while they are occurring.

Emotional management: Emotional management encompasses your potential to control the feelings you assert so that they stay reasonable to a given circumstance. Becoming skillful at emotional power requires that you cultivate skills such as maintaining perspective, calming yourself down, and shaking off out-of-control irritability, anxiety, or sadness.

Self-motivation: Self-motivation involves your ability to keep your litigations goal-driven even when distracted by emotions. Self-motivation inevitably includes being able to delay satisfaction and avoid acting in irrational ways.

Empathy: Empathy involves your capacity to study and adequately discern other people's needs and wants. The trait that contributes to altruism is empathy, which is your ability to put others' needs ahead of your own needs.

Relationship Management: Management of relationships requires the ability to predict, consider, and react appropriately to others' emotions. It is closely associated with empathy.

These various skills work together to form the basis of emotionally intelligent behavior. With numerous strengths and weaknesses, people come to the challenge of emotional intelligence.

Where some find it easy to develop self-awareness and empathy, others have a hard time or don't grasp the need quickly. Just as emotional resilience, emotional intelligence can be nurtured and built. To strengthen your emotional, physical, and social well-being, you can learn how to work with emotions properly.

About the Author

MANNING L. CROMER is a graduate of Philosophy (Bachelor of Arts). A specialist in Hospitality Human Resources and Management with over eighteen years of hotel experience in human resources and development. He has worked with various international hotel chains in different countries in Asia-Pacific Region and the Middle East. He has also delivered countless lectures on personality development and has held various seminars on management skills and customer services.

Manning L. Cromer is a personal and emotional growth counselor due to his diverse human emotional expression experience. He uses this open-mindedness in his writing and sheds light on how the power emotions can be harnessed and wielded right to withstand life's curveballs.